Earth

by J.P. Bloom

ABDO
PLANETS
Kids

abdopublishing.com

Published by Abdo Kids, a division of ABDO, PO Box 398166, Minneapolis, Minnesota 55439.

Printed in the United States of America, North Mankato, Minnesota.

102014

012015

 THIS BOOK CONTAINS RECYCLED MATERIALS

Photo Credits: iStock, NASA, Science Source, Shutterstock, Thinkstock

Production Contributors: Teddy Borth, Jennie Forsberg, Grace Hansen

Design Contributors: Candice Keimig, Laura Rask, Dorothy Toth

Library of Congress Control Number: 2014943797

Cataloging-in-Publication Data

J.P. Bloom.

 Earth / J.P. Bloom.

   p. cm. -- (Planets)

ISBN 978-1-62970-715-0 (lib. bdg.)

Includes index.

1. Earth (Planet)--Juvenile literature. 2. Solar system--Juvenile literature. I. Title.

550--dc23

                2014943797

Table of Contents

Earth

Earth is a **planet**. Planets travel around stars. Planets in our solar system **orbit** the sun.

5

Earth is the third closest **planet** to the sun. It is about 93 million miles (150 million km) from the sun.

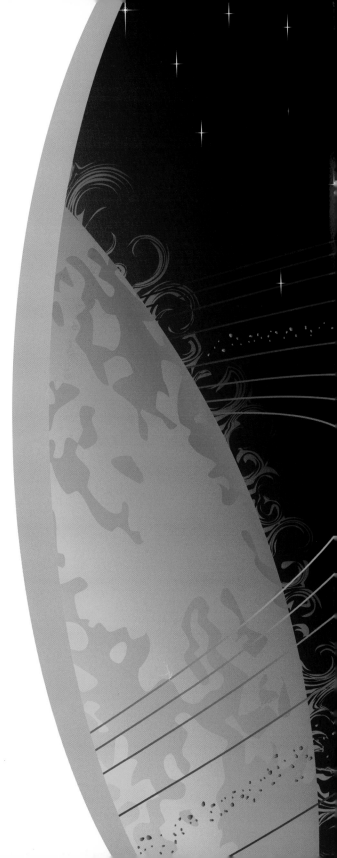

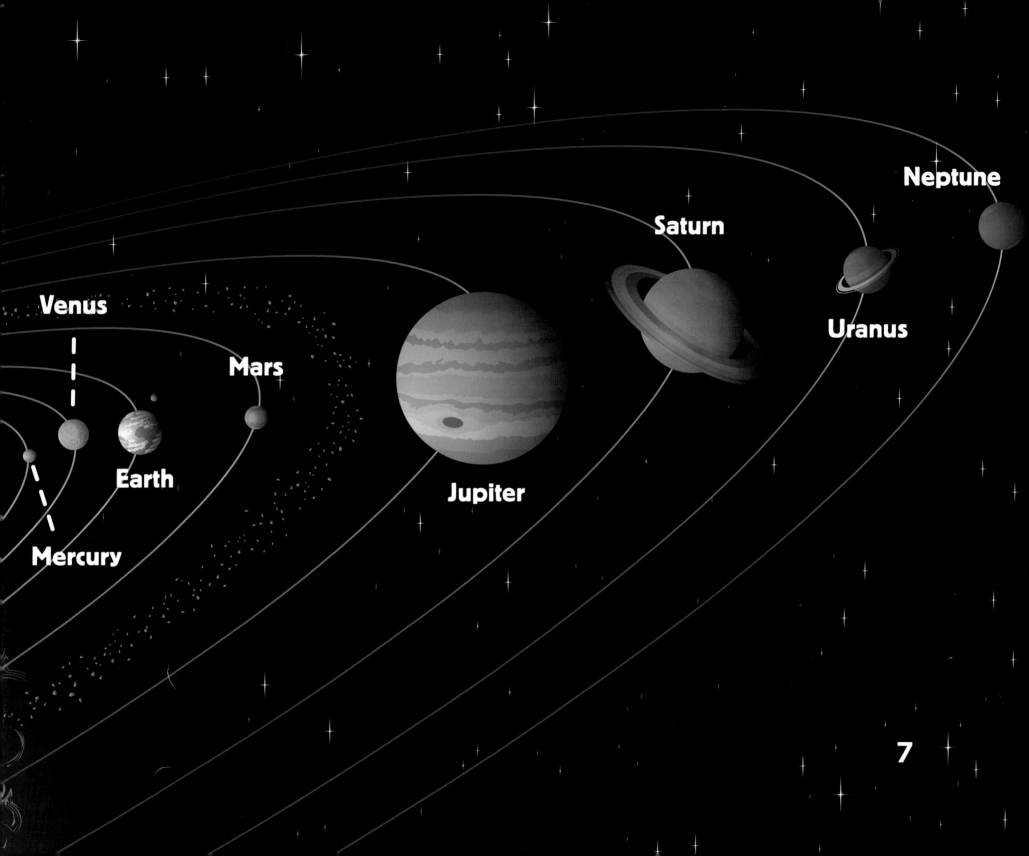

Earth **orbits** the sun every 365 days. That is equal to one year.

9

Earth spins while it **orbits** the sun. One full spin takes 24 hours. The spin makes day and night.

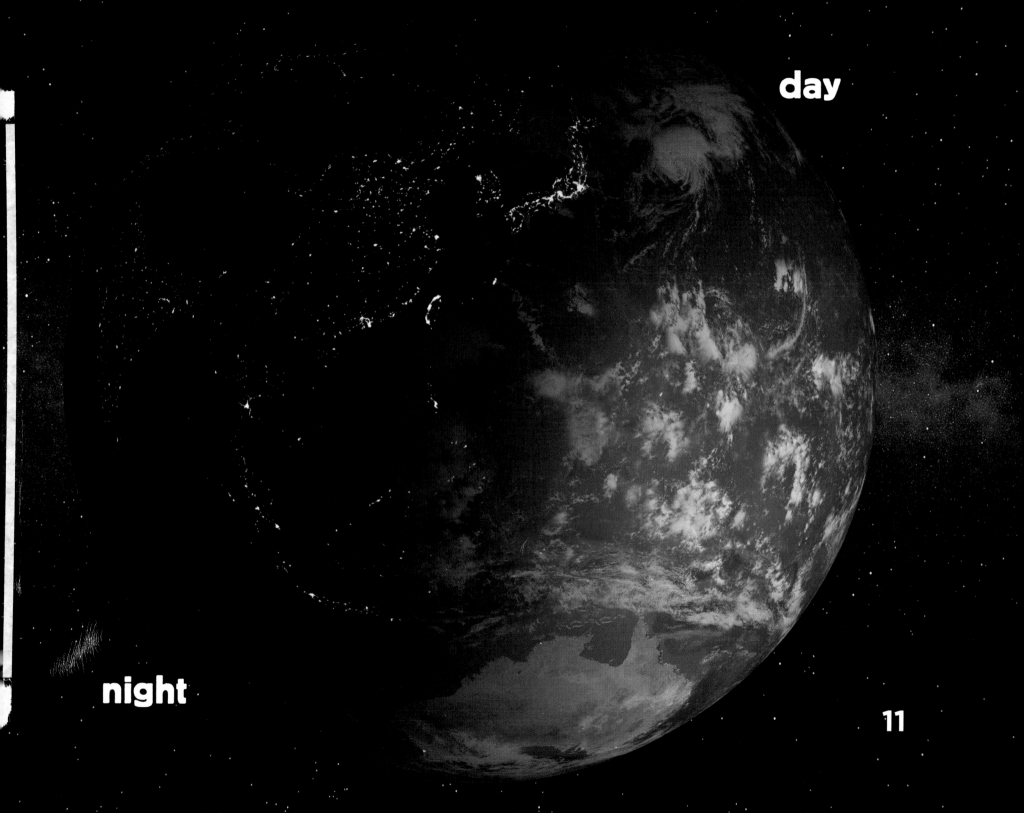

Earth spins on an **axis**.

Earth's axis is tilted.

The tilt creates the seasons.

Summer

Autumn

Winter

Spring

13

Earth is made of three layers. They are the core, mantle, and crust.

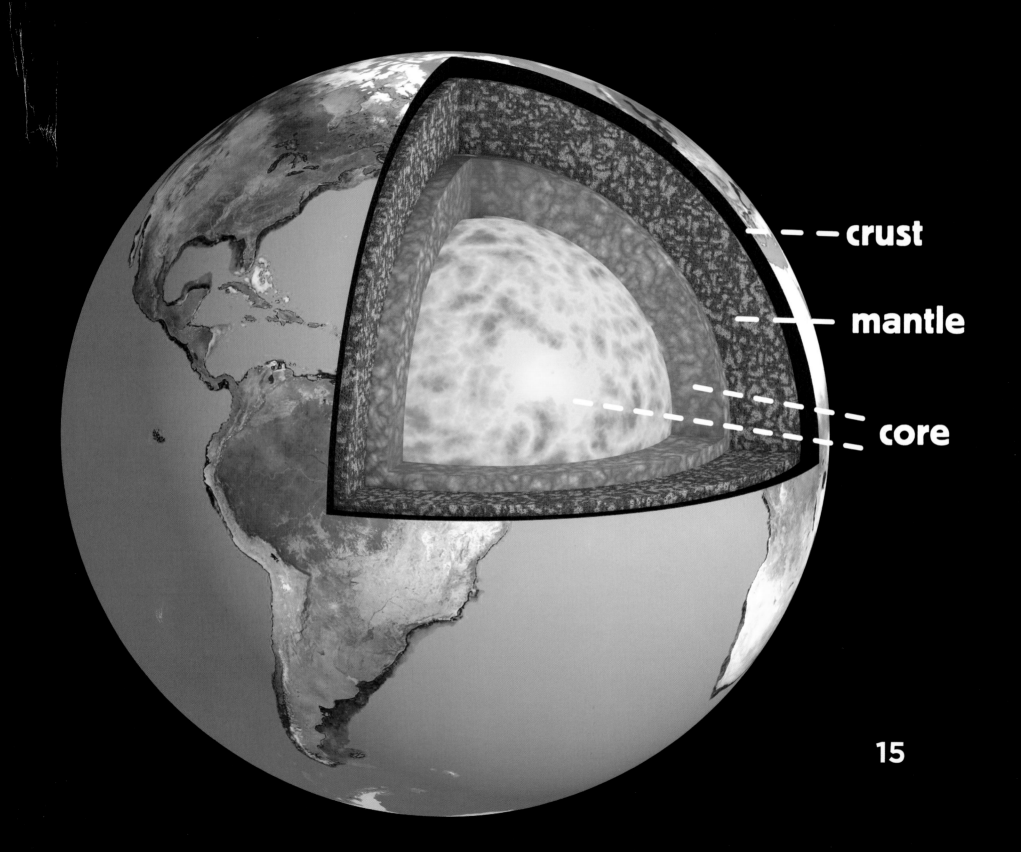

crust

mantle

core

15

Water, Land, and Air

Water covers 70% of the earth. Earth has 7 landmasses called continents.

North America

South America

Europe

Asia

Africa

Australia

Antarctica

Earth's atmosphere is made of gases. It is made mostly of **nitrogen** and oxygen. Living things need these to breathe and live.

19

Life on Earth

People, plants, and
animals live on Earth.

More Facts

- Earth is the only **planet** known to have life. Over 7 billion people live on Earth.

- Living things need water. If Earth were closer to the sun, the water would dry up. If it were further, the water would freeze. Earth's place in space and **orbit** make it a perfect planet for life.

- Earth is the only planet in our solar system with plate tectonics. Tectonic plates move and collide underground. This process recycles carbon, which keeps Earth from getting too hot.

Glossary

axis – an imaginary line through a planet. Planets spin around this line.

Nitrogen – a colorless, odorless gas that makes up about 78% of Earth's atmosphere.

orbit – the path of a space object as it moves around another space object. To orbit is to follow this path.

planet – a large, round object in space (such as Earth) that travels around a star (such as the sun).

23

Index

abdokids.com

Use this code to log on to abdokids.com and access crafts, games, videos, and more!

Abdo Kids Code:
PEK7150